THE ENGLISH GENTLEMAN'S MISTRESS

THE ENGLISH GENTLEMAN'S MISTRESS

Douglas Sutherland

INTRODUCTION BY
LADY WINDLESHAM (PRUDENCE GLYNN)

DRAWINGS BY
TIMOTHY JAQUES

DEBRETT'S PEERAGE LTD

Published by Debrett's Peerage Ltd
73/77 Britannia Road, London SW6

ISBN 0 905649 45 1

Printed and Bound by
Robert Hartnoll Ltd., Bodmin, Cornwall.

We wish to thank Tom Hartman, Alexandra Culme-Seymour and Carol Illingworth for their editorial and social advice on the most delicate volume in Debrett's history. The two hundred years of documentation and research into the Aristocracy has also been used, and much appreciation is due to the editors past and present.

Contents

Introduction
by Lady Windlesham (Prudence Glynn) 9

Chapter 1 19

Chapter 2 25

Chapter 3 31

Chapter 4 45

Chapter 5 57

Chapter 6 67

Introduction

INVITED to supply an introduction to this latest exposé of the habitat of an undoubtedly endangered species, my first thought was that it would be great fun. My second was that it would be impossible. English gentlemen simply do not have mistresses. Edward VII? He was at least three-quarters Hun, and certainly not a gentleman. Edward VIII? Marginally less of a Hun simply by dint of having been over here for longer but considered by many to be an effeminate bounder – fancy wearing your top hat at the wrong angle when out with the Quorn. Lloyd George? Common little Welshman, of course he doesn't count; especially since he sought to buy himself into the upper classes by selling titles to other non-gentlemen. Bertrand Russell is somewhat more promising material, what with poor Mr Whitehead knowing all about it (a third party suffering always makes it *much* more fun), but although undoubtedly of gentlemanly birth, Russell was an intellectual and thus deeply suspect to other English gentlemen. Indeed, his voracious love life with Mrs Whitehead came about while they were burning the candle at both ends over *Principia Mathematica*.

The reason that most English gentlemen do not have mistresses is threefold. Firstly, they are too mean. Secondly, they are undersexed. Thirdly, they have no need whatever of the status symbol of wealth or position which is implicit in keeping an obviously very expensive piece of property for display purposes and with a very low return on your investment, at any rate in public.

The difference, you see, between a tart or between a live-in girl friend as they are now called, with all the lack of romance and connotations of washing the socks and even if necessary having to fork out for the gas bill (Women's Lib has a lot to answer for), and a mistress is that mistresses are *kept*. English gentlemen are, quite surprisingly, prepared to take tea at the Ritz, as afternoon adultery is referred to in this country. In France the pastime is known as *le cinq à sept*, the hours between leaving the office and having to report home. The point is that, in France, the little one is waiting in a chic apartment provided by her admirer. She has spent the day with her couturier, hairdresser, lingerie maker and shoemaker, to be sure to be perfectly pleasing when He arrives, cross and tired, but nevertheless all set to ravish. He will also have paid for the couturier, hairdresser, etc.... In England, if the gentleman did actually take tea at the Ritz one would probably get landed with the bill.

A previous Lord Hertford, it is true, is said to have paid a million francs for the pleasure of one night with Virginie Oldoinin, *maîtresse-en-titre* of Napoleon III, in 1855. But he seems to have got his money's worth. Determined, with true English commercial/aristocratic good sense, to make sure that 'no volupté was withheld', he submitted the Countess to such an *embarras d'amour* that she had to spend the next three days in bed. Resurrected, her rivals were furious to notice that she looked more beautiful than ever.

As to lack of sexual drive in gentlemen, this is easily explained by the fact that most of them drink too much, and alcohol, though it diminishes the inhibitions inculcated by their upbringing, is a rotten sexual stimulant. Debutantes in fear of what remains of their honour in taxis should just get their escort, already reeling, even more tight in the basement flat. Gentlemen have many other ways of dampening their sexual ardour – going out shooting all day, or hunting, or serving as a magistrate, or opening things – all occupations calculated to induce a desire to 'turn in early, old thing', or to go to sleep at the dinner table rather than flirting with the newest blonde divorcee in the county. Scottish gentlemen will have an advantage when deer ranching takes off, since there is no reason to suppose that the powdered horn of the stag should be any less effective as an aphrodisiac than that of the rhino. They will have to move fast to beat the Chinese in their demands but, on the other hand, the Norwegians, who are already into deer-ranching, use it for powdered soup. Now we know how they survive those interminable, long, dark Nordic nights, but I suspect that the object of their attentions is not in true terms a mistress.

This plethora of occupations among English gentlemen explains why their ladies form liaisons with their gamekeepers or clear off to hoe the herbaceous border. It also explains why English women are regarded on the Costa Brava as a 'Good Thing'.

The third reason is that the gentleman does not need to prove his wealth or position in society. As a great man, encountered in St James's Street in a distinctly tatty overcoat, remarked, 'In the country everyone knows who I am, so it does not matter; in London nobody knows who I am, so it does not matter'. Arrivistes might need to parade the rungs of the social and financial ladder by way of an exceptionally expensive mistress. Not the English gentleman who, far from displaying his *poule de luxe*, tucks her away behind tea-cosy lampshades somewhere very dull.

Do English gentlemen still have mistresses? Only if they are very rich, or if they have an expense account. 'Have you met my new secretary / personal assistant / archivist / housekeeper?' are phrases to alert the gentlewoman, even if employed on a commercial occasion. Some gentlemen do have to lend their names to commercial writing paper in order to keep the ancestral roof over their heads, so why not a V.A.T.-free perk or two? Gauche non-gents scurry around without such proper introductions – 'This is Mrs X.' Fatal because in country life everyone wants to know just who fits in where, and in commercial life everyone knows that the firm is footing the bill for the box at Ascot and All Must Be Chargeable.

Singing hey, dilly-dilly dilly, come and be filled,
For you must be delighted and my Company billed.

Alcohol. . .is a rotten sexual stimulant

There is, even now, a certain demand for English women as mistresses in the true sense. The cognoscenti keep a list of possible protectors, and when one gets tired of his current incumbent they look at that list and see to whom she has not yet been handed. Complications occurred not so long ago when the short list of possible takers-on was consulted – the lady, though beautiful, was somewhat past her prime and quite remarkably boring – only to reveal that out of the six suitable candidates she had already been the property of five. Consternation, but not complete. Number six, rich, insecure and naïve, took her on – and then married her. But then he was neither English or a gentleman. And now he has another mistress.

On the whole, English gentlemen do not marry their mistresses. It upsets the children, who loathe them, however tiresome Mummy may have been, it horrifies the servants when the *Daily Express* or Dempster ring up and the master says, 'She is not here' when Mrs Danvers has just found knickers all over the bathroom, and it leads to frightful rows about the tiara and Granny's pearls. If an English gentleman does marry his mistress, she is almost certain to be Austrian or South African or some such, and has thus no hesitation in blackmailing her gentle, gullible catch by means of the aforementioned yellow press.

Much as I love Douglas Sutherland, he could give the less resilient cause for inferiority. Perfectly sure in my place as a gentlewoman, he has pointed out that if I aspired to be a lady I should fail the 11-plus; half of my most charming relations have got some very dodgy accreditations as gentlemen.

But it is best to know oneself, and I know that I should have been a perfectly hopeless mistress, then or now. Instead of lying on the sofa eating peppermint chocs in my tea-gown and waiting for the sound of the key (after all, it would be his house) in the lock, or better still, the rustle of the footman's kneebreeches (always far too tight, saucy monkey) as he let in the lord and protector, I should have felt it my duty to be ladling out soup to the poor, or enquiring into the working conditions of the seamstresses who were blinding themselves for my latest toilette or my lover's shirts. Hardly an ideal background for a little fun and games. Rather the cross face refusing to wear aigrettes in my hat or bandeau on the grounds that they are an endangered species, cruelly obtained and remorselessly destroyed. Of course, at the turn of the century, dear Queen Alexandra would have been on my side – she refused to wear them – and I should have been a member of the Audubon Society of America.

The most appalling aspect would have been that the men who did keep mistresses were generally palpably plain, and had some very nasty habits. My dictionary, the Lady's Dictionary, naturally was not able to inform me of the meaning of coprophilia, a prominent interest of one Alfred Edwards, supposedly the richest man in Paris, when Madame Natanson was sold to him to pay her husband's debts. Mind you, she was not just the most fascinating lady I have encountered in biography. No wonder that Marcel Proust used her schizophrenic charms as a model for two leading characters in *À la Recherche du Temps Perdu*. Toulouse-Lautrec's poster for *Reine de Joie* by Victor José is more explicit than a dozen porn windows in Soho.

And then one would have been expected to entertain them and generally jump around and put butter on the floor and have pillow fights in order to alleviate the ennui of the lifestyle which warranted mistresses. Conversation was invariably coarse: they would have thought that Stravinsky was a sure bet for the Derby. And I simply could not cope nowadays, what with having to wash up and getting dumped with the bills and then persons overdosing all over the carpet.

But then, you see, I am English and thus am subject to the ruling of the greatest Madame of modern times, Madame Claude. Naturally, as the supplier of discreet delights to every taste and race, provided they can pay, she resides in Paris. Arrested finally, despite the obvious embarrassment caused to many highly-placed figures, Madame told *Lui* magazine that to succeed, 'One must shine in three fields; beauty, intelligence and, to simplify matters, bed. I turned down ravishing young women, handsome as the night, because the very excess of their beauty would have prevented the exercise of their art with all the rigour required.' Oh goody, there is hope for us all if Madame is out of jug. She is! I see she was merely fined £1,000, a soupçon, one imagines, compared to the prices she charged her highly selective clientèle.

Of we native Brits, Madame had this to say.

'English girls are disconcerting, unexpected, and full of fantasy. I rarely presented an English girl to staid or rather mournful men. The outcome was always disastrous. An English girl who is not amused always ends up by treating as a bore the partner who has not known how to make her smile.'.

All the way to the bank?

LADY WINDLESHAM (PRUDENCE GLYNN)

I

What shall we do, my-soul, to please the king,
Seeing he hath no pleasure in the dance?

LORD ALFRED DOUGLAS

UNTIL the death of King Edward VII it had, for several hundred years, been the custom in this country for Royal Family to set the tone of fashion. When we think of the reign of a particular king or queen we think at once of the lifestyle dictated by the court. This was as true of the prevailing moral standard as it was of what the ardent seeker after fashion wore, what he ate, what he played, even what he thought – when he did. In this brief survey of the English gentleman's mistress, therefore, let us start by having a look at the example set by a few illustrious royal personages.

For this purpose it is not necessary to go back too far in time. Indeed, to do so would be to enter into highly conjectural realms, anathema to the dedicated historian.

There is one school of thought, for example, which insists that Queen Elizabeth I took a distinguished series of lovers, most of whom were subsequently parted from their heads on the block in the Tower of London, while another school insists that the balding, gravelly-voiced, moustachioed monarch was really a man in drag, and a homosexual to boot. Either way, there does not seem to be much support for the public image of the Virgin Queen.

Nor does the track record of her father, Henry VIII, throw much light on the scene. The fact that he married a considerable number of wives and literally gave a couple of them the chop is only an earlier variation on the later Elizabethan theme.

It is when we come to Charles II that things look up a bit. For little Nell Gwynne must go down in history as one of the finest plumes in Charles's royal bonnet. When she ousted that infinitely boring French woman, Louise de Kéroualle, from the royal favour it was a very popular home-win indeed with the British public, and a particularly sharp lesson for mistresses in general, and Louise in particular, that they should keep their noses out of politics. This is a path that even wives should fear to tread, as Marie Antoinette was later to discover.

Nell managed to give every satisfaction without even bothering to learn to read or write. But she was certainly a realist, as is clearly shown by her remark when her carriage was surrounded by an angry crowd during the 'Popish Terror' of 1681. 'Good people,' she cried out, 'let me pass. I am the *Protestant* whore.'

'Let not poor Nellie starve', Charles, much to his credit, is said to have commanded his brother from his deathbed in 1685, and nor did she. James gave her a fine estate near Nottingham, and her eldest illegitimate son was made a duke. In fact the dynasties founded by both Nell and Louise de

Kéroualle survive to this day, personified, respectively by their Graces the Dukes of St Albans and of Richmond and Gordon.

But Nell did not survive her royal master long; she was only thirty-seven when she came to be buried at St Martin's-in-the-Fields in 1687. Nevertheless she had done much to gild the image of the perfect mistress.

It was an image which was to be swiftly tarnished by the arrival on the scene of the cumbersome Hanoverians. The great British public could readily forgive George I for his inability to learn English and for his spending more time in his native Germany than in his adopted country, but they found it hard to overlook the succession of unattractive, middle-aged hausfraus he brought with him to share the royal bedchamber on his rare visits to our shores.

Hausfraus. . .to share the royal bedchamber

The Prince Regent started off much better by marrying, albeit secretly and illegally, the beautiful and estimable Mrs Fitzherbert, before running true to form and marrying yet another approved mare from the seemingly inexhaustible Hanoverian stables.

William IV, while Duke of Clarence and waiting to occupy the throne, whiled away the time having five daughters and five sons by the long-suffering Mrs Jordan, an extremely talented actress who seldom made a stage appearance without it being obvious to the audience that yet another royal bastard was on the way. After he had discarded her, she fled from her creditors to France where the bold William allowed her to die in penury.

It was royal examples such as these that made the whole business of having a mistress rather unfashionable with the British upper classes of the time. We might have been able to beat the French on the battlefield but we could not compete in the bedroom.

Even the elegance of the Regency stopped short of the bedroom door. The bucks of the day seemed to be much more concerned with playing the peacock in the smoking room of White's Club than in the boudoir.

It was not until Edward VII, as Prince of Wales, took the stage that virility came back into fashion. While his mother swathed herself in ever more voluminous weeds of mourning, Edward started out on a course of extramarital dalliance which was eventually to restore the mistress to her

. . .much more concerned with playing peacock

proper place in the social order.

But let us now digress by making a short trip to France where the habit, indeed the art, of keeping a mistress attained a perfection never really achieved on this side of the channel. The French have most surely made much progress since Shakespeare saw fit to remark that 'It is not the fashion of the maids of France to kiss before they are married.'

2

L'amour est l'histoire de la vie des femmes;
c'est un episode dans celle des hommes.

MADAME DE STAËL

In any serious study of the role of the mistress, such as this, we must pay tribute to the race who, by their own unashamed admission, spend more working hours in pursuit of love than are ever lost by industrial action in more prosaic lands – the French.

One must resist entering into a discussion on the rival merits and status of the great royal courtesans such as Mesdames de Pompadour, Récamier, or Dubarry, lest their careers of meteoric brilliance blind us to the more pedestrian role of the mistress in the upper échelons of French society.

With typical French sensitivity, extra-marital liaisons are generally described as *alliances de la main gauche*, but it is very much a case of the right hand knowing what the left hand is doing, for the taking of a mistress by a French gentleman is a very serious matter indeed for the whole family, and not a situation to be entered into lightly. In a way it confers a certain status, like buying an expensive watch by Cartier.

The main difference between the two is that a

really good Cartier watch requires virtually no maintenance, but the same cannot by any means be said of even the least demanding of mistresses.

Pas Devant Les Enfants

It is not often that a young French gentleman takes a mistress. He feels happier roistering in the bordellos of Montmartre while courting a suitable bride, and continues to do so, if marginally more discreetly, after marriage.

It is only with an acceptance of the passing of the years that he feels the need to settle down, to establish his place in society, and to undertake the responsibilities which are expected of him. It is at this stage that he starts looking round for a mistress.

The Wife–Mistress Syndrome

By and large, it is not done for a Frenchman to take a friend's wife as a mistress. His delicacy in this respect is in sharp contrast to the American way of life and a few degrees more circumspect than his peers in British and German society.

On the other hand, it is not unknown; but a French gentleman so placed would feel it his duty to inform his friend of the fact.

I can remember dining in a well-known gentleman's club in Paris with two very gentlemanly Frenchmen. As we sipped a fine old Armagnac, one turned to the other and remarked conversationally:

'By the way, *mon brave*, since we are such old friends I feel I owe it to you to tell you that I am sleeping with your wife.'

I froze, my glass poised. Surely, I thought, this was the classic case of pistols for two and breakfast for one. Not at all.

'Indeed, *mon cher ami*,' replied the other, looking at his friend with great interest. 'Tell me. Is she any good at it nowadays?'

This case must be regarded as the exception rather than the rule.

An Arrangement of Convenience

It is more usual for the French gentleman to find an unattached lady and, once found, to set her up in circumstances of reasonable comfort. It is accepted that the more beautiful she is, the greater the prestige reflected on her patron.

The arrangement is never furtive. Although the wife will not acknowledge her existence publicly and will take great pleasure in cutting her, in the unlikely event of their meeting in public, it will not stop her approving privately of her husband's choice, and she will even allow her children to be asked to tea and sticky cakes by the mistress.

If this may seem very strange to wives in more permissive societies it is, in fact, founded on logical reasoning.

A Code of Conduct

As in other aspects of French society, there are very strict rules of protocol governing the position of the mistress.

She must, for example, never bee seen with her patron in any public place where her presence is likely to prove an embarrassment to the wife, such as the opera, the enclosure at the races, the first day of an exhibition, or a couturier's private view, even though she may buy her clothes there.

At the same time she must remain entirely faithful – a condition which, as we have seen, does not always apply to the wife.

She should really try very hard, subject to the

Every token of affection bestowed on the mistress. . .

proper religious observances in a predominantly Roman Catholic country, not to have children. To do so not only complicates an otherwise simple situation but disrupts normal services.

Most important of all, the mistress must never win vis-à-vis the wife. That is to say it is a point of honour with the French gentleman that every token of affection bestowed on the mistress, however expensive, shall be visited on the wife sevenfold. In this respect a mistress can be re-

. . .shall be visited on the wife sevenfold

garded as a positive necessity in any well-ordered family circle. How else could a wife whose husband's passions have cooled extract those gewgaws so near to every woman's heart?

It is indeed a wise wife who asks for the key to the family safe immediately after the mistress's birthday. Her excuse is that she must send the family heirlooms for their annual cleaning. In truth, of course, it is to check that no little trinket is missing. Husbands, knowing this, accept it with resignation.

An additional bonus to the mistress system in France is that the French have one of the lowest divorce rates in the western world.

So, you see, the whole thing really works very well indeed. Except possibly for the mistress.

3

> 'I shall not say why and how I became, at the age of fifteen, the mistress of the Earl of Craven.'
>
> HARRIETTE WILSON, *Memoirs*.

TO RETURN to our main theme, as we have already observed, it was largely due to the strenuous efforts of the Prince of Wales, later Edward VII, that, in the second half of the nineteenth century, the English gentleman's mistress became established as part of the social scene.

Although the English gentleman had a fairly free passport when it came to establishing an extra-marital relationship, there were, as in France, certain conventions to be observed. Victorian, and later Edwardian, Society would tolerate almost any sort of behaviour, providing everyone played according to the rules.

In the case of mistresses, the rules were very simple. No ostentatiously rich gifts, no public appearances of the mistress with her benefactor. To get your mistress pregnant was regarded as the height of carelessness but not to make adequate financial provision for any offspring the height of caddishness.

In the normal course, a gentleman would expect to call on his mistress at the same time every day, usually on his way home from luncheon at his club – unless, of course, he had an out-of-town commitment at somewhere like Newmarket or Ascot. It was only required of him that he should be home in good time to change for dinner.

Should, for any reason, this convenient arrangement be interrupted, it was understood, if he was dining alone with his wife, that he could leave the table early. It was the convention to explain that he had an engagement to make up a four at whist at his club, even if it was well known that he never touched a card.

It was not, however, acceptable that he should have both an afternoon and an evening appointment on the same day, it being considered under these circumstances that the mistress was getting more than her fair share.

At the same time, the attitude of the upper classes towards promiscuity amongst their social inferiors was one of the utmost disapproval. Indeed, for a second footman to be caught making calf-eyes at a lady's maid was to court instant dismissal.

There was an incident reported from the Earl of Lonsdale's magnificent family seat, Lowther Castle, towards the end of the last century which perfectly demonstrates this attitude.

Lady Lonsdale's personal footman, while rashly attempting to gain access to a lady's maid's bedroom, fell off a drainpipe and crashed through the glass roof of a conservatory below. He was instantly dismissed, not for the damage he had done, but for what he had intended to do.

. . .making calf-eyes at a lady's maid was to court dismissal

One of the favourite occupations of ladies left with too much time on their hands was to sit on committees to discuss the problems of immorality among their social inferiors, and even that pillar of respectability, William Ewart Gladstone, took a great deal of time off from being Prime Minister to carry out practical research among fallen women.

It should be noted here that the ladies who eventually achieved the status of an English gentleman's mistress were invariably not of the same high social standing as their patrons. It may well, therefore, be asked how, in such a well-regulated society, gentlemen were ever able to meet possible mistress material?

The answer lies in the accepted practice of allowing young gentlemen of good family, between achieving puberty and being expected to lead a suitable bride to the altar, to sow their wild oats; hence the very vulgar expression of 'having your oats'. For this purpose there were several meeting places of low repute in the West End of London which it was regarded as acceptable for young men to visit.

Notable in this category were the Argyll Rooms at the bottom of Shaftesbury Avenue and 222 Piccadilly, more generally known as 'The Pic' or 'The Three Bloody Twos'.

The acceptance of this custom was not without risk so far as society mothers and their marriage-hungry daughters were concerned, for it was inevitable that there should be a certain amount of wasteage amongst the ranks of eligible bachelors.

The most dangerous waters, so far as the

marriage brokers were concerned, was the Holborn Casino, where the standard of beauty among the hostesses was exceptionally high. Harry Vane Millbank's father gave him £10,000 on condition that he gave up the idea of marrying a leading beauty from the Casino. Young Millbank took the money, but there were others who did not get away. Kate Cooke, Rose Wilson, and Valerie Reece, all Casino 'girls', became respectively the Countess of Euston, Lady Verner, and Lady Meux, while eligible young society ladies ripped their cambric handkerchiefs to shreds in frustration.

It makes an interesting footnote to the history of Edwardian mistresses that not all were dazzled by the possibility of a brilliant marriage. Emma Crouch, for example, preferred to play the field. Adopting the *nom d'amour* of Cora Pearl, she cut a swathe through the upper échelons of Europe's richer aristocracy and managed to earn and spend a reputed £15,000,000 during her undisputed reign.

By and large, however, it was from the ranks of old flames of their heydays that gentlemen were able to find a congenial mistress with whom to grow old gracefully.

Not all gentlemen were prepared to keep their mistresses discreetly in the background, particularly if they were outstandingly pretty and amusing.

An example was Lord Fitzwilliam, who allowed his pert and pretty mistress, Caroline Walters, unusual latitude in meeting his friends.

Caroline Walters was universally known as 'Skittles'. It is said that she earned her nickname in the back streets of Liverpool where she started her career setting up the pins in a skittle alley, before coming to London to seek her fortune.

It was Fitzwilliam's delight to show her off each morning during the Season, mounted on one of his superb horses, in the daily parade in Hyde Park of those wishing to see and be seen. To watch the quality ride by was one of the few free entertainments open to the poor and they were exceptionally knowledgeable about who was who. Skittles' appearance was the signal for much wolf-whistling and the passing of loud comments which she accepted regally as her just due.

It is worth recounting here another of Skittles' triumphs because it was the sort of thing that was the very stuff of upper-class gossip.

Her prowess on a horse was remarkable, so much so that Lord Fitzwilliam allowed her to turn out regularly with the fashionable Quorn Hunt. This sparked off the most intense rivalry, much to the delight of the hard-riding hunting fraternity, between Skittles and Lady Stamford, wife of the Master.

To add to the piquancy of the situation, Lady Stamford's own origins were somewhat suspect. It was rumoured that she was of gipsy origin and that before her marriage had been 'in competition' with Skittles. Arrogant and overbearing, she sought to impress everyone in sight with her social position. As one of the hunting bloods once remarked of her, 'You can never satisfy a woman who is accustomed to nothing'.

The rivalry between the two reached its climax at an opening meet of the Quorn when Lady Stamford, taking a leaf out of the book of the famous Duchess of Montrose, turned out in an eye-catching habit of blue velvet. Hearing of this, George Fitzwilliam fitted out Skittles in an even more dazzling outfit of bright scarlet – a choice of colour which was not lost on a highly amused field. Lady Stamford, however, was not amused.

Using her authority as wife of the Master, she ordered Skittles home in front of the whole field. She reckoned, however, without Lady Grey, who was also at the meet, and who at once arranged for Skittles to change into more conventional attire at her nearby hunting box and then rejoin the hunt.

Delight knew no bounds when, at the end of the day, Lady Stamford asked the identity of the young lady who had ridden so well in front of her all day, only to discover that it was her hated rival.

As has been remarked, however, such splendid confrontations between an established wife and an established mistress were the exception.

In making this observation it should not be assumed that a gentleman confined his attentions outside the family only to his mistress. This was very far from the case. Led by the example of the Prince of Wales, most gentlemen in the upper échelons of society also sought further amorous diversions inside their own social circle. It should be realized, however, that this was largely on a catch-as-catch-can basis and seldom led to any permanent liaison.

Nocturnal sport

It was for this reason that the Edwardian house party in the country enjoyed such immense popularity. House parties were ostensibly given for shooting or some other outdoor activity, but it is true to say that it was the indoor games to which the guests looked forward most keenly. This nocturnal sport was admirably summed up by Hilaire Belloc thus:

There will be bridge and booze 'till after three,
And after that a few of them will grope
Around the corridors in *robes de nuit*,
Pyjamas or some other kind of dope.

These affairs took a great deal of careful planning on the part of the hostess. Not only had she to make sure in advance which ladies the more important guests would like to be invited, but she also had to ensure that the after-midnight traffic in the darkened corridors upstairs was carefully regulated so that there were as few collisions as possible.

Some years ago a very elderly Dowager described to me how the very first house party at which she was hostess after her marriage nearly led to her social ruin.

The lady in question was one of the prize-winners in the Great American Invasion of the 1880s and 1890s when rich heiresses from our erstwhile colony over the water carried off many of our more impecunious aristocrats.

It would have seemed that, soon after her glittering wedding, the seal of approval had been set on the match when the Prince of Wales accepted an invitation for a shooting weekend at her husband's country seat.

Alas for the course of true love, she had not done her homework properly. The first indication she had that all was not as well as it should have been was when, shortly after midnight, the drawing room, which a moment or two before had been a-buzz with happy chatter, fell ominously quiet. The reason was not far to seek. Looking around, she found the room to be deserted save for a couple of very elderly and evidently very discontented gentlemen. Finding that the expected post-midnight entertainment had not been organized in advance, they appeared to be at the point of coming to blows over who would be the recipient of their hostess's favours. Just when it was coming to the point when she feared she was to be torn in half, the argument was interrupted by a bellow of rage from the floor above. The traffic upstairs, which had been steadily building up, had reached its peak about eighteen minutes after the time of retiral, as would have been expected by a hostess of greater experience.

With no proper traffic control, the inevitable had happened. One guest, proceeding in one direction down the corridor, hands outstretched in front of him to give warning of any unexpected obstacle, had encountered another guest proceeding in the opposite direction. That the object the startled man now found himself grasping so firmly turned out to be the Imperial beard was, not to overstate the case, unfortunate.

One is also reminded of the story of Lord

Charles Beresford, the famous 'Charlie B', as well known in the corridors of concupiscence as in the hallowed halls of the Admiralty, who missed his way in the dark one night, opened the wrong door and, with a cry of 'Cock-a-doodle-doo!', leapt into bed, only to find himself between the Bishop of Leicester and his wife.

. . .with a cry of 'Cock-a-doodle-doo!'

By and large, however, in Edwardian Society everything was very well arranged indeed. There was a time and a place for everything, which is in sharp contrast to our present higgledy-piggledy way of life. There was none of this modern democratic business of Jack being as good as his master, and certainly no question of his mistress being as good as Jack.

However, it must not be imagined that it was only in the rarified social atmosphere of the grand Edwardian house party that shooting and hunting provided a suitable front for amorous dalliance. Coming a rung or two down the social ladder, one does not need an interpreter to explain why the followers of a certain well-known pack of otter hounds were known on the Welsh Marches as the Love and Luncheon Club.

Edwardian Society was self-sealing. To elevate oneself from one social stratum to another was extremely difficult. It is a curious fact that the reason why this is no longer so is largely due to Edward VII's pioneering spirit. Edward positively encouraged social climbers, not only in his choice of men friends but of his lady friends as well. Sir Philip Magnus gives us a neat vignette of his Coronation: 'Inside the Abbey, in a special King's box dubbed irreverently "the King's Loose Box", the presence of a number of King Edward's special friends, including the actress Sarah Bernhardt dressed in white, Mrs Hartmann, Lady Kilmorey, Mrs Arthur Paget and the reigning favourite, Mrs George Keppel, excited hushed wonder and admiration.' Lady Frederick Paget described

Sarah Bernhardt as 'a woman of notorious, shameless character'; Mrs Hartmann was the daughter of an Alsatian chemist who had made a fortune in the Lancashire textile trade; the Countess of Kilmorey was a lady of undistinguished birth whose circumstances had been much enhanced by marriage; Mrs Paget and Mrs Keppel, however, both sprung from respectable and respected stock.

One of the most indefatigable social climbers of Edward's day was the wealthy American widow, Kate Moore, who was for a time one of his regular dining companions. As one wit remarked on hearing of Kate's death, 'Ah! This will be a great night for Kate; no doubt she will be dining with God.'

4

'The Western custom of one wife and
hardly any mistresses . . .'
SAKI, *A Young Turkish Catastrophe*

WHEN, after Edward VII's death, Queen Alexandra returned to Lily Langtry a not-so-little pile of her monogrammed handkerchiefs which she had, over the years, left behind in the Royal bedroom, perfectly laundered and with a letter of sympathy over their common loss, it was to be hoped that the place of the mistress in Society had been established once and for all. Alas, not so.

On the contrary, with the death of the King Emperor the mistress as an upper-class status symbol gradually fell into decline so that today she is high on the list of endangered species. Of course, there are still a few dedicated preservationists amongst our aristocracy, but the ranks of the stalwart rearguard are becoming thinner year by year. It was therefore with particular pleasure that I read in the *News of the World* – keen observers of the species will have observed that the English gentleman always finds an excuse sometime on Sunday to visit the servant's hall. This is in order to read the *News of the World* – as I was saying, I read in the *News of the World* as recently as February, 1979, the following statement made by

FINANCIAL TIM

Milo, 18th Viscount Hereford and Premier Viscount of England: 'Surely it is customary for a man to have a mistress. I had several before I got married, and then had my first again four years after my marriage. Altogether, since then, I've had four.' Bravo, Lord Hereford!

But the sad fact is that Lord Hereford is a giant in a land of pygmies; and where does the blame lie for this dismal situation? The answer, I fear, is that much of the blame must lie on the collective doorstep of British womanhood.

The writing was on the wall even before the Second World War. Of course, there were still mistresses aplenty in the carefree, cocktail-drinking, Charleston atmosphere of the 1930s, but every now and again there would be a chill reminder to the perceptive observer of the social scene that society was dancing on its own grave.

To the Manor Born

Let me give an example of the sort of thing I mean. There was a noble and elderly Earl of my acquaintance who was a pillar of respectability in one of our more remote backwoods. His married life set an example of domestic bliss to the tenantry, and every Sunday they stood respectfully while he and his large family took their seats in the front pew of the village church.

That for many years he had kept a mistress in a modestly comfortable little house in a neighbouring village (to have her living on his own land would, of course, have been *quite* wrong) was both acknowledged and accepted. Indeed, if anything, the very tidiness of the situation added to his reputation as a good father and devoted husband.

Then, inconsiderately, his wife of some thirty years' standing died. The only matter for speculation in the village was how long might be considered a decent interval before he moved his paramour into the big house and made an honest woman of her. When, instead, he married the widow of one of his neighbouring landowners, the whole locality was outraged. Even his mistress locked her front door against him, and there were few who could be found to disagree with her.

Of course they were all quite wrong in adopting this censorious attitude. A decade earlier, nobody in their right mind would have expected a chap to marry his mistress just because his wife had become dead. Once a mistress, always a mistress. It goes to show how rapidly standards had declined since the days of Edward the Peacemaker.

Young Macdonald Had A Farm

Another example of the insidious growth of middle-class morality in the interwar years concerns a tenant farmer on my family estate. He too was happily married and the measure of his marital felicity was that each year, as surely as the sprouting of his wheat crop, his wife would give birth to yet another sturdy bairn.

Macdonald was, however, a man of great virility. He also kept a mistress and, each year, as surely as the reaping of his harvest, she, too, would add her contribution to his rapidly expanding family. Mrs Macdonald had a great deal to put up with, particularly as she was required to look after both sets of children, but I must record that she was as shrewish as the mistress, untrammelled as *she* was with the cares of rearing a family, was delightful.

Then, after only twelve years of marriage and a total of twenty-one siblings to show for it, Mrs Macdonald passed on.

Unlike my noble friend, whose matrimonial adventures I have already described, Macdonald bowed to popular opinion. His mistress became the second Mrs Macdonald. The result could have been predicted by anyone accustomed to the *mores* of those of higher social rank. Overnight the new Mrs Macdonald completely changed her spots. No sooner had Macdonald slipped the ring of respectability on to her finger than she became arrogant and domineering, flaunting her changed status on every possible and impossible occasion. She soon became a pillar of the Church, ostracizing anyone who she suspected of committing the deadly sin of adultery.

As for Macdonald, he soon realized his error. He waited only long enough to bring the total of his dependants up to twenty-two before leaving to join his first wife in the great beyond. One can only hope that he found her, relieved of the cares of motherhood, in a better frame of mind.

A Salutary Lesson

I tell this cautionary tale at some length to demonstrate that it behoves us all, of whatever social degree, to think very carefully before listening to moral arguments against the time-honoured rôle of the mistress, and I might gently point out here that it is largely women who clamour for a change in the *status quo*.

Decline and Fall

The decline of the mistress gained greater momentum with the outbreak of the Second World War. Up to that moment in our island history, which spelt destruction for so many of those things which people of my generation held dear, mistresses in certain areas were still pretty thick on the ground.

Even so, it was obvious that change was in the air. For example, the phrase 'a dirty weekend' had become current. It was used, and still is for all I know, to describe a weekend of illicit love, usually in some seaside resort such as Brighton, or up the Thames in inappropriately-named places like Maidenhead.

Of course, the term 'weekend' should be sufficient indication in itself that this was no upper-class activity. Ladies and gentlemen go to the country from Friday to Monday or whatever may be the appropriate period: never for 'le weekend', a term that has been adopted by the French, who like to poke fun at our English morality.

As for the term 'dirty', with its overtones of guilty, extra-marital activity conducted behind the drawn blinds of some anonymous boarding house, this has never been the gentleman's style. In the Edwardian era, as we have observed, house parties in gentlemen's country houses provided, and

His mistress became the second Mrs Macdonald

'a dirty weekend'

indeed were often designed to give, an opportunity for amorous dalliance. Many gentlemen lived their whole lives without ever staying in an hotel, and certainly not an hotel in Brighton or Maidenhead. To take their wives to lunch or dine at the Ritz or the old Berkeley on their birthdays was as much as most of them used to manage.

The Ubiquitous Salesman

The dirty weekend, so beloved by the manufacturers of saucy postcards, was invented by the middle-class husband stifled by the oppressive, relentless respectability of places like Penge; the excuse they made to their wives for leaving them behind was traditionally that they had to attend a sales conference and would be under such pressure that they could spare no time for social niceties. To salve their consciences they would usually bring their wives home some token of their affection, such as a stick of Blackpool rock. I do not believe that even today it is a practice that has been adopted to any extent by gentlemen.

Time Flies

St John's Wood, and even Maida Vale, have long since lost their once-thriving mistress population. The reasons for this are largely economic. Indeed, with central London becoming progressively seedier, it makes more sense for anyone in a position to afford a mistress to reverse the geography of the Edwardians by living in style in St John's Wood and keeping his mistress in Mayfair.

The Old Cavendish

The raffish reputation once enjoyed by hotels such as Rosa Lewis's Cavendish in Jermyn Street is no more. Indeed, the Cavendish, which during the whole of Rosa's long reign never to my knowledge saw a pot of paint, is now a gleaming, multi-storied hotel geared to the needs of modern man, where the ghosts of Rosa and her lifelong companion, Edith, must roam uneasily.

The process of erosion at the Cavendish had set in long before it fell into the hands of the developers. It was said by the post-war generation that Rosa, like some female King Canute, resisted the incoming tide to the last. Sons of former habitués were in the habit of boasting that she would arrange that the bills of those whose fathers she had known and approved of should be added to the bill of some *parvenu* of whom she did not approve. I can only say that although I was always greeted as a long-lost friend, her ageing eyes never grew less shrewd and my bills rose to a level that was positively eccentric. Perhaps it was simply because she did not like Daddy, but I doubt it. Now I shall never know.

When The Lights Went Up Again

The fate of the Cavendish was by no means unique. By the time the lights of London went up again in 1945 quite a few had been extinguished for ever and in many of the haunts of the 'thirties where a gentleman might be expected to take his mistress rather than his wife the wick had burnt so low that it was obvious the oil must soon give out.

'Ma' Meyrick had served her last prison sentence for serving unlicensed drink to her aristocratic customers. The Café de Paris, where so many of the witty, the pretty, and the rich had made their dramatic entrances down the famous double staircase, was a bomb crater, and the stage-door

. . .they would usually bring their wives home some token of their affection

Charlies no longer drank champagne out of actresses' slippers in Romano's.

The day of the mistress was quietly drawing to a close and the voice of Women's Lib was about to be heard in the land. Women's Lib indeed!

5

The old order changeth, yielding place
to new,
And God fulfils himself in many ways,
Least one good custom should corrupt
the world.

ALFRED, LORD TENNYSON,
The Idylls of the King

IT WOULD be less than gallant of me to lay the entire blame for the virtual eclipse of the gentleman's mistress on womanhood as a whole and women's libbers in particular.

The truth of the matter is that it is mainly to the financial policy of successive post-war Governments that one must look when seeking to apportion the blame.

There are, of course, other factors like the rapacity of landlords which makes the maintenance of two establishments in London quite out of the question; the fact that a gentleman cannot claim tax relief in respect of maintaining a mistress is one of the great social injustices of our time.

Inequality of Opportunity

By comparison with the lot of the gentleman, observe how the top-level business executive is favoured in our materialistic society when it comes to the matter of mistresses.

Private Relations Officer

All the high-powered businessman has to do is put his mistress on the company's pay roll under some such title as 'P.R.O.' which, it need not be explained to the accounts department, does not stand for Public but Private Relations Officer.

Alternatively, he can hire her in a freelance capacity, which has the advantage that he can reclaim the V.A.T.

A gentleman, of course, would have a strong moral scruple against charging up his mistress, even if he had the faintest idea how to do it.

Changing Terminology

I have already remarked that in the good old days, if a gentleman did not actually boast about his mistress, at least he did not seek to hide her, either literally or metaphorically, under the bed.

Nor for that matter did the mistress. If, glancing at the pub clock and seeing that it was later than she thought, she would hurriedly down her port and lemon, excuse herself from the company by saying that she was expecting her gentleman caller, everyone would nod knowingly.

Indeed, a great deal of time was spent by ladies discussing the rival merits of their gentleman callers over thimblesful of port and lemon. His generosity, his family background, and his style of dressing and undressing all came in for the closest examination and comparison.

All that has changed now. Gentlemen friends went out with gas-lit street lamps. Now, even the term 'lover' is outdated. The sexes seem to be divided into birds and blokes, regardless of the degree of intimacy or marital status.

Of course, if some particularly titillating scandal implicates a well-known public figure, inevitably some Sunday newspaper will pay a huge sum of money for the aggrieved lady's memoirs, which will almost certainly be entitled 'I was his Sex Slave'.

While we are discussing terminology, I am reminded of a story about that distinguished journalist Mr Frank Giles, whose wife, Lady Kitty, was the daughter of Earl de la Warr. Mr Giles had been interviewing an American businessman who, when the interview was over, suggested that he and his wife should join him for dinner. Mr Giles accepted the kind invitation and as the American rose to leave he said, 'Well, goodbye Mr Giles and I look forward to seeing you and to meeting Mrs Giles this evening.' Now Mr Giles had married an earl's daughter, a fact that was not to be lightly disregarded. So he said, 'Well actually, she's not *Mrs* Giles. . . .' but, before he could explain, the American said, 'That's quite all right. Bring her anyway. Used to keep a little woman myself once.'

Sexual Deviationism

There seems to be a generally-held belief that gentlemen who have had the dubious benefit of a Public School education inevitably emerge as either sadists or masochists.

I do not entirely subscribe to this view, although there are undoubtedly quite a large number of ladies who make a fairly decent living

The aggrieved lady's memoirs

YOUNG LADY GIVES STRICT SPANISH TUITION
SCHOOL MISTRESS WELCOMES NEW PUPILS
LESSONS IN CORRECTITUDE
STRICTURAL ENGLISH
THE STORY OF O LEVELS
FOR SALE SCHOOL UNIFORM
BANGER FOR SALE
GOVERNESS GIVES ADVANCED TUITION
ANYTIME SWITCHED ON
JANE THE CANE

beating the hell out of elderly Peers of the Realm, Bishops, and so on.

My objection is that this is not a curiosity limited only to members of the upper classes. If the great number of advertisements in the windows of the sleazier newsagents is anything to go by, half the adult population of London is at it.

Nor, by any stretch of the imagination, are the ladies who describe themselves as 'strict French mistresses' etc., mistresses in the true sense; they can therefore be disregarded in any serious study of the subject.

At the same time, it would be equally wrong to assume that the mistress is purely an invention of the upper classes. It is true to say, however, that the English gentleman can take the credit for making the mistress respectable.

The stories concerning the amorous adventures of everyone from travelling salesmen to window cleaners are legion, but they lack the cosy permanency of the gentlemen's arrangements.

Pension Fund

It might be noted here that a gentleman's mistress of long standing would normally expect a reasonable pension after she retired from active service, and to be remembered in her benefactor's will. This is a far cry from the deplorable modern practice of discarded mistresses having recourse to the Courts to extract suitable compensation.

One further observation on the changed circumstances of the mistress demonstrate only too clearly how an unsympathetic series of Governments has destroyed their way of life.

In the good old days the English gentleman's mistress took great pride in her job. The visit of her gentleman was the highlight of her day and her interest in his doings and in those of his family her main inspiration. She would even cut out pictures of his wife, should her photograph happen to appear in one of the glossy magazines, and paste it carefully in her scrap-book. Indeed, decline in circulation of society magazines over the years has been in direct ratio to the decline in the number of *bona fide* mistresses. This is just another thing for which our political masters must, in the final analysis, bear responsibility.

But there is worse to come. Even if one has to accept the passing of the old order, there are certain aspects of the new order which no gentleman could tolerate without a sharp rise in blood pressure.

Of course, it has long been accepted that among those classes without the means to maintain a full-time mistress, a certain amount of discreet sharing is permissible.

For example, a mistress lucky enough to live in a town which is on an established travelling salemen's circuit might with perfect propriety entertain Jones the Toothpaste on Mondays, Harry the Ladies' Lingerie on Tuesdays, Bill the Insurance on Wednesday's, and so on, happy in the knowledge that she is giving all her gentlemen value for money.

Now, however, there are indications that the big business tycoons who spend their lives jetting

. . .paste it carefully in her scrap-book

round the world are coming to somewhat similar arrangements. While many gentlemen have had to face up to the fact that in the present economic climate it is inevitable that they should have to syndicate their pheasant shoot, to resort to similar measures in respect of their mistress is the ultimate in the unacceptable face of capitalism.

Surely if there is any section of the community today which deserves the sympathetic support of the Small Businesses' Association it is the grossly exploited Band of Mistresses.

6

'With heigh! the sweet birds, O, how
they sing!
Doth set my pugging tooth on edge.'
WILLIAM SHAKESPEARE,
The Winter's Tale

WHEN women's liberationists made a funeral pyre of their brassieres and rose from the ashes twittering like a flock of excited starlings, there was much muttering into moustaches in some of the remoter parts of the country about what the devil things were coming to.

Of course, most of the mutterers had reached an age when what women did with their bras was a matter of purely academic interest. All the same, there were quite a few thinking men who were seriously worried as to whether the ladies, God bless 'em, were acting in their own best interests. One likes to think that they represented the rearguard of the gentlemanly brigade. It was only the cads who relished the prospect of having to pay only their share of a night out on the tiles as a prelude to putting up token resistance to an Amazonian attack in the back of a taxi on the way home.

What, it may be asked, were the advantages of being a mistress which, by and large, have been so lightly thrown away?

. . .glowing and radiant for the ring at the door

There were many, but I will content myself with listing only the more obvious ones.

The most appealing to the average woman must be that the role of mistress gave her security without responsibility. In a way, it was like being head girl in the harem without the competition.

If it is conceded that the subject nearest to a woman's heart is whether she is looking her best for whatever tasks the day may involve her in, the mistress is at a great advantage over her sisters. Consider the plight of the career lady, required to look neat but fetching for the office, a trifle more farouche for that pleasure-mixed-with-business luncheon, and, after an hour battling through the home-bound rush hour, positively glowing and radiant for the ring at the door that announces the arrival of her heart-throb for the evening.

The mistress is required only to occupy herself with such weighty matters as the length of her eyelashes or whether to change from crushed strawberry to coral nail varnish.

Even a gentleman's lawful married wife has far greater pressures to put up with than his mistress. Consider, for example, the dreadful worry of deciding whether hubby's new Ford is as acceptable as a status symbol as the next door neighbours' Japanese job. Consider the agony of trying to make polite conversation to the dinner guests whilst wondering if the roast in the oven is burning away to a frazzle; and when the children start to make their appearance, and nanny after nanny gives in her notice; and when her husband's new-found passion for contract bridge drives her to a state of neurosis wondering if she is going to remember the Blackwood four/five no-trump convention.

Ah, lucky lucky, mistress. Like the lilies of the field, she toils not neither does she spin.

But, of course, these are the familiar plaints of the embattled housewife. It may be that it was this line of argument which set the match to the fuse that set off the women's lib detonation; in which case it is only a question of deciding whether the explosion took place too late and whether there were any mistresses left to blow up.

The Importance of Adultery

Obviously, there are many factors to consider before attempting to make any sort of head count of the existing mistress population. The water is considerably muddied by the current fashion of disregarding the sanctity of marriage. Whereas not many years ago women spent most of their waking hours plotting how to get the man in their life to pop the question, now they merely mutter something about 'Who wants a piece of paper anyway?' before slipping between the sheets. If a chap neglects to marry the woman with whom he is living, how can he possibly claim to have a mistress on the side? Nor can he boast of having two mistresses and no wives. A mistress is essentially a violation of section seven of the Ten Commandments as laid down in the Book of Common Prayer. It is quite clear that no man can commit adultery unless he is married.

On the other hand it can be argued that, in

Making polite conversation to the dinner guests

these permissive days, even in places like Wychwood-on-the-Water or Much Soddington, it would be hard to find enough virgins over the age of consent to make up a ladies' four at tennis on the Vicarage lawn. Again, this is of no great significance. Promiscuity in itself does not a mistress make.

This narrows the field down to those people who can not only afford it but also have the opportunity of forming at least a semi-permanent adulterous relationship. Most gentlemen nowadays do not qualify on either count. No longer do they find themselves at a loose end every afternoon, and their financial difficulties have already been discussed at some length in this work.

The Honorourable Member

If most gentlemen are no longer starters in the Mistress Stakes, then who are?

Even the most casual observer of the social scene cannot fail to recognize that Members of Parliament, of all Parties, must come high in the ratings. This does not necessarily mean that our legislators are any more randy than the rest of us. It is simply that they, by the nature of their occupation, spend most of their working days exposed to the temptations of life, in the capital, while their wives are left in some remote part of the country chatting up the constituents.

From the number of Members who can be observed dozing off in the Chamber during the day, it is tempting to draw the conclusion that many of them are not getting enough undisturbed sleep at night but, of course, it could be simply a built-in defence mechanism against having to listen to the wearisome speechifying of some of their colleagues.

. . .The wearisome speechifying of some of their colleagues

Spies

By contrast, there is another sector in which an ability to sleep around would appear to be an essential qualification for the job. Mata Hari did not rise to the top of her profession by sitting behind an office desk. The recent revelations of the strange sexual habits of some of our more upper-class spies does nothing to alter the generally held belief that there are plenty of red-blooded 007s whose working clothes are not the traditional cloak and dagger but an elegant silk pyjama top.

It is only a matter for debate because the professional aspect of their work may render their amateur status forfeit and, therefore, of course, they cannot qualify as gentlemen.

The Good Old Days

Perhaps in this changing world it is as well to accept that the good old days when everybody knew their place above or below the salt are gone for ever.

Oh, bitter pill to have to admit that the aristocracy is no longer to be found lunching in St James's, strolling on the hallowed turf of the Royal Enclosure, or taking the big fences in the hunting field.

Instead, the cries of the market place are to be heard in the land. But does the demise of the English gentleman mean that his mistress must also be swept away in the avalanche?

Dare we hope that in some far corner of our green and pleasant land there still lurk a few of the pure-bred species? Is there still some manorial estate where the wicket gate is left open so that the nocturnal comings and goings of the master can pass unobserved?

While the dwindling numbers of the Red Kite and the Hen Harrier are a matter for universal concern, is there no one who will pass round the hat on behalf of the Society for the Preservation of Gentlemen's Mistresses?

I hope so. Oh, I do hope so.

JAQUES